Tiddalick

Written by Isabel Thomas

Illustrated by Annie Wilkinson

RISING ★ STARS

One day, Tiddalick the giant frog woke up feeling very thirsty. He hopped to the lake and began to drink.

He drank and drank and drank, until the lake was dry.
"That's better," thought Tiddalick, "but what if I get thirsty again?"
He decided to find more water.

Tiddalick hopped slowly to the river and began to drink. He drank and drank and drank, until the river was dry.
Now the giant frog was so full of water, he could hardly move.

But Tiddalick never wanted to be thirsty again.
So he trudged to the waterhole and drank the
water there, too.

Other thirsty creatures arrived at the waterhole.
"Our lake is dry," said Snake and Kangaroo.
"Our river is dry," said Kookaburra and Koala.

"Oh no!" said Echidna. "The waterhole is dry, too."
"I've solved the mystery," said Wise Owl. She
pointed at the huge frog sitting by the waterhole.

"Tiddalick has taken all the water for himself."

"Please open your mouth," said Kookaburra. "We are all thirsty. If we don't drink soon, we will die."

Tiddalick shook his big head, and kept his huge mouth shut.

"We must get the water back," said Kangaroo.

"Let's make Tiddalick laugh," said Wise Owl.
"Then he will have to open his mouth."

"I'll try first," said Kookaburra. "I am an expert at laughing." He puffed up his chest, opened his beak, and laughed his loudest laugh.

Ha
Ha
Ha
Hee
Ho!

But Tiddalick did not laugh.

"Let me have a go," called Kangaroo.
She tickled Tiddalick under the chin with
her long, ginger tail.

Tickle
Tickle
Tickle

But Tiddalick did not laugh.

"I know what to do," said Wise Owl.
She turned her head all the way around ...
and back again!

But Tiddalick did not laugh.

"I can do better than that," said Echidna.
He rolled in the dry leaves until they stuck to every
bristle. The other animals thought it was funny.

But Tiddalick did not laugh.

"I'll try a funny dance," said Snake.
She flipped and flopped. She wiggled and waggled.
Tiddalick did not laugh. But Snake kept trying.

She made silly shapes. She twisted and turned.
She tried so hard that she tied herself in a knot!
"Oh no!" cried Snake.

The other creatures tried to help Snake.
They tugged and heaved. They wrestled
with the knot.
At last, Snake came loose with a POP!

Pop!

Suddenly, the creatures heard a noise.

Tiddalick was trying not to giggle.

A tiny drop of water leaked out of his mouth.

It fell on to the dry, dusty ground with a PLOP!

Plop

Next, Tiddalick began to chuckle. Finally, he roared with laughter. Water gushed out of Tiddalick's mouth.

It poured into the waterhole.
It flowed into the river.
It filled up the lake.

The dry land became green once again.
That day, Tiddalick learned the most
important rule of nature.

Take only what you need, and no one
will go without.

Talk about the story

Answer the questions:

1 What type of animal is Tiddalick?

2 What did Tiddalick drink first?

3 Why did the other animals want the water back?

4 Why did the animals want to make Tiddalick laugh?

5 How would you make Tiddalick laugh?

6 What do you know about the different animals in the story?

Can you retell the story in your own words?